A GOVERNMENT TA health care syste more plausible.

Support for the idea is at an all-time high, according to Gallup. Two-thirds of Democratic voters favor it; even one in four Republicans is on board. "Medicare for All" bills have been introduced in the House and Senate, with record numbers of cosponsors.

Senator Bernie Sanders has emerged as one of the dominant forces on the political left, thanks in part to his call for "single-payer" health care. That call was the linchpin for his 2016 presidential campaign. The passion his supporters exhibited for single-payer has prompted many leading Democrats around the country to embrace the idea.

WHAT IS SINGLE-PAYER?

Under single-payer, a single entity pays for health care services. The only entity with the heft to shoulder that responsibility is the government.

If single-payer were to take hold in the United States, private insurance coverage would be outlawed. About 160 million people who get health benefits through work – roughly half the population – and more than twenty million people who purchase insurance on their own would lose their private coverage and have to enroll in a new government-run plan.

Supporters of single-payer claim it can ensure universal coverage for significantly less than a privately administered system. A single government insurer doesn't have to spend money on marketing. Its administrative costs may be lower, given its scale. And as the only buyer of health care, it can theoretically drive a hard bargain with doctors, hospitals, and drug companies.

Outside the United States, single-payer is the norm. The United Kingdom's National Health Service was the world's first single-payer system; it formally launched in 1948. Almost all doctors and nurses in the United Kingdom work directly for the NHS.

Canada, too, has a single-payer system. Health care providers don't technically work for the Canadian government, but it retains exclusive rights to cover services defined as "medically necessary." Doctors cannot accept

---

Single-payer's siren song is appealing. Who wouldn't want free, universal coverage that eliminates premiums, deductibles, and copays? Unfortunately, the reality of single-payer doesn't comport with that promise.

---

payments for such services from patients; they must bill their provincial government.

Even in the United States, certain segments of the population – seniors, the poor, military veterans – are subject to single-payer.

Its siren song is appealing. Who wouldn't

want free, universal coverage that eliminates premiums, deductibles, copays, provider networks, complicated bills, and the like?

Unfortunately, the reality of single-payer doesn't comport with that promise. Long wait times, substandard care, lack of access to innovative treatments, huge public outlays, and spiraling costs are endemic to single-payer.

PART I

SINGLE-PAYER NIGHTMARES IN CANADA AND THE UNITED KINGDOM

Those pushing for a government takeover of the US health care system argue that the United States is the only developed country that doesn't guarantee health care to its citizens – and that every other country spends less for better-quality care.

"I live 50 miles south of the Canadian border," said Senator Bernie Sanders, the pied piper of single-payer health care. "For decades, every man, woman and child in Canada has been guaranteed health care through a single-payer, publicly funded health care program. This system has not only improved the lives of the Canadian people but has also saved families and businesses an immense amount of money."

But the supposedly "free" care offered by countries like Canada comes at an extremely high cost.

Patients living under single-payer are subject to long waits for subpar care and shortages of everything from cutting-edge medical technology to hospital beds. These outcomes are the natural product of government-run systems that struggle to keep costs under control.

To paraphrase former British prime minister Margaret Thatcher, socialized health care systems abroad are running out of other people's money – and are rationing care as a result.

Oh, Canada

I spent the first four decades of my life in Canada – and can say firsthand that the picture Sanders paints bears little resemblance to reality.

Canada's health care system is defined by its waiting lists. In 2017, Canadians faced a median wait time of 21.2 weeks between referral from a general practitioner and receipt of treatment from a specialist, according to the Vancouver-based Fraser Institute.

That's more than double the 9.3-week wait the typical Canadian faced in 1993, when Fraser began tracking wait times.

Sanders should know as much. Danielle Martin, a Canadian doctor and supporter of single-payer, told the senator in a September 2017 interview, "We do have a problem with wait times for what we call elective or non-urgent procedures."

Yet Sanders implored Canadians in October 2017 to "be a little bit louder" in their defense of their health care system. Only 64 percent of Canadians say they're proud of their health care system.

The waits in Canada aren't just for minor procedures. Canadians routinely queue for months, often in pain, for heart surgery and knee transplants. In November 2017, a family doctor in Ontario reported that one of her patients was facing a four-and-a-half-year wait to see a neurologist.

There are more than eighty-five thousand people – almost 2 percent of the population – awaiting surgeries in British Columbia,

A quality health care system does not prompt people to seek care abroad on their own dime. Last year, more than sixty-three thousand Canadians sought health care outside the country.

according to the province's own data. Nationwide, more than one million people – nearly 3 percent of Canadians – were waiting for procedures in 2017, according to the Fraser Institute.

If you apply that same rate to California, some seven hundred thousand people – all of whom would nominally have health coverage under single-payer – would be on a wait list. That's greater than the population of the state's capital, Sacramento.

The Canadian Institute for Health Information says that 20 percent of Canadians have to wait a week or more to see a family doctor. Wait times for emergency room treatment are longer in Canada than in ten other industrialized countries, according to the Commonwealth Fund.

Canadians have to wait for diagnostic tests as well. In its 2017 report, the Fraser Institute found that the median wait time for a CT scan in Canada was more than four weeks. For an MRI, it was almost eleven weeks; for an ultrasound, just under four weeks.

Bed Blockers

Why the long waits? Despite Canada's universal coverage guarantee, the country has too few doctors, hospital beds, and diagnostic machines to adequately care for its citizens.

Canada has fewer doctors relative to its population than all but seven nations in the Organisation for Economic Cooperation and Development, a group of thirty-five developed nations. It's tied for second to last in acute-care hospital beds per one thousand people. Canada is also in the bottom third for

MRI machines and CT scanners per person.

Canada appears to think it can save money by limiting the supply of care. But those limits cascade throughout the health care system and exacerbate costs elsewhere.

Consider long-term care facilities. Canada doesn't have enough of them, according to a 2016 report from Health Canada. Many seniors stay in the hospital longer than clinically necessary because there's nowhere else to go.

Indeed, as the *Edmonton Sun* reported in January 2017, "At any given time, around 400 hospital beds in Alberta (one-third in Edmonton) are taken up by bed-ridden seniors waiting for placement in long-term care/nursing home/assisted-living facilities." These seniors are stuck in hospitals for sixty-nine days, on average.

One report has called this phenomenon "hospital gridlock." Because hospital beds don't open up when they should, patients have their surgeries cancelled, wait longer in the emergency room, and experience worse health outcomes, according to Health Canada.

Poor Outcomes

Despite Canada's promise of universal coverage, it fares poorly on measures of health outcomes. A Commonwealth Fund survey of eleven developed countries ranked Canada ninth in overall performance.

Advocates of single-payer counter that the United States fared even worse in that report — dead last. But that's largely a product of how poorly the United States fares on measures such as infant mortality and longevity.

Countries each measure infant mortality differently. Belgium, France, and Spain, for example, register live births only when the baby has lived for a specified period of time beyond birth. Those babies who don't survive aren't included in infant mortality statistics.

The United States, by contrast, deems all babies who show signs of life immediately after birth as live births. America also delivers many more premature and low-birth-weight babies than do other countries. These babies are unfortunately more likely to die – and thus skew US infant mortality statistics.

Longevity rates are heavily influenced by societal and lifestyle factors like rates of drug abuse, obesity, car accidents, and crime. It's hard to conclude that the US health care system is worse than Canada's because more Americans die prematurely due to homicides or drug overdoses.

A far better measure of the quality of a health care system is how patients fare after they enter the hospital or doctor's office. On that score, Canada performs worse than the United States.

The death rate in hospitals for patients suffering a heart attack is 22 percent higher north of the border. It's almost three times as high for those suffering a stroke.

Survival rates for people with breast, colon, lung, and prostate cancer are also lower in Canada. The five-year survival rate for US breast cancer patients is 89 percent, compared to 86 percent in Canada. For prostate cancer, the five-year survival rate in the United States in the United States is over 97 percent; it's just over 91 percent in Canada.

Further, a quality health care system does not prompt thousands of people to seek care abroad on their own dime. Last year, more than sixty-three thousand Canadians went outside the country to get everything from orthopedic surgery to radiation treatments.

Indeed, the United States has become Canada's health care relief valve. Canada's leaders don't mind. Every Canadian who pays for treatment out of pocket abroad is one more Canadian who doesn't need his government to pay for his care. That's a win for the Canadian treasury.

Here's just one example. My cousin's father-in-law, an investment banker in Canada, was told that he needed heart surgery but would have to wait two years before he could undergo his procedure. Fearing for his life, he flew to the Cleveland Clinic in Ohio and paid out of pocket for the life-saving procedure.

If the United States were to adopt a single-payer system, where would Canadians – not to mention Americans – go for timely care?

High Costs

Canada's attempts to control costs by limiting the supply of care aren't working. Between 2001 and 2016, spending by Canada's provinces on health care shot up 116.4 percent. Health care now consumes anywhere from 34 percent to 43 percent of provincial budgets. A 2010 study showed that health costs in Ontario were on track to comprise 80 percent of the province's budget by 2030.

Taxpayers must shoulder these costs. Canada's "free" health care now costs families anywhere from $4,000 to more than $12,000 in taxes, according to the Fraser Institute.

Worse, these costs have been growing faster than the country's economy. Between 1997 and 2017, the cost of Canada's government-run program climbed 173.6 percent, which was nearly twice the growth of Canadian incomes – and four times the rate of inflation.

> *"Illegal" private clinics like Canada's Cambie Surgery Centre perform sixty thousand surgeries per year on patients who choose to pay for their own care.*

And these are just the visible costs. Wait times impose their own indirect costs. Fraser calculated the cost of waiting for care at more than $1.7 billion in 2016. That estimate is based on the value of productivity lost during the average workweek.

That's a conservative estimate. It doesn't include expenses borne by families who care for relatives while they wait for treatment – or costs Canadians incur when they travel abroad for care.

What's more, the Canadian single-payer system doesn't cover dental care, vision care, long-term care, or prescription drugs. Most

Canadians have to buy private insurance for these services.

In fact, private insurance covers 15 percent of Canada's health care costs, according to the Organisation for Economic Cooperation and Development. Out-of-pocket spending accounts for another 15 percent.

Suing for Private Insurance

The situation in Canada is so dire that some patients and doctors are suing to import some measure of private, American-style health care. In British Columbia, orthopedic surgeon Brian Day is leading a suit that seeks to allow private insurers to pay for care that the law gives the public system the exclusive right to cover – and to permit doctors to bill patients privately. Both practices are currently illegal.

Private clinics like Day's Cambie Surgery Centre perform some sixty thousand surgeries per year. The patients paying for those procedures don't need the government to pay for their care. That saves the government some $300 million a year, according to Day.

The case is currently playing out before British Columbia's Supreme Court. If the plaintiffs win, British Columbia could have a real alternative to single-payer – and could set a precedent for the rest of the country.

There have been other cases like Day's in Canada. In the 2005 *Chaoulli v. Quebec* decision, the Canadian Supreme Court struck down the ban on private insurance – but only in Quebec. It also did not address whether doctors should be allowed to bill patients directly for procedures covered by Canada's single-payer system.

Trouble in the United Kingdom

The United Kingdom's health care system differs in some ways from Canada's. For instance, Britons are allowed to carry private insurance alongside their government coverage; about 10 percent do.

The UK government's promise is the same

as Canada's — free, universal health care. And just as in Canada, that promise has gone unfulfilled.

Rationing

In 2017, the United Kingdom's National Health Service (NHS) attracted international attention when two of its clinical commissioning groups (CCGs) — local health authorities responsible for planning and commissioning health care services for their area — announced that anyone who was overweight or a smoker would be denied nonurgent surgery. The two groups collectively cover 1.2 million people.

Under the rules, smokers have to quit for at least eight weeks before being allowed in the operating room — and undergo a breath-alyzer test to prove it. Patients who have a body mass index over thirty are required to cut their weight by 10 percent before being considered for surgery.

One of the CCGs said that the new policy was "the best way of achieving maximum value from the limited resources available."

It's rationing, pure and simple.

The *Independent* in London has reported that "an increasing number of CCGs are using similarly discriminatory policies. Other recent policies had required patients to be in varying degrees of pain, while some CCGs had imposed bans on surgery for several months to save money."

In January 2018, the NHS ordered as many as fifty-five thousand nonurgent operations cancelled or delayed for at least a month in order to free up space and time for urgent and emergency care.

According to NHS figures, patients suspected of having colon cancer often face a three-month wait for a colonoscopy – a procedure the NHS says should be done within six weeks. The NHS also found that 26,113 patients waited longer than three months after being referred by their general practitioner for "urgent" cancer treatment.

Health service regulators found that 3.7 million Britons, out of a population of 65.6 million, wait longer than eighteen weeks for surgery. That figure is expected to climb to 5.5 million by 2019.

Shortages of Everything

Britons wait largely because shortages pervade the NHS. As in Canada, the government does not have the resources to pay for all the care patients need.

There were seven thousand fewer doctors in the United Kingdom in 2015 than in 2005 — even though the country's population grew by 5.2 million. In 2017, there were more than thirty thousand open positions for health care providers. There was also a shortage of about forty thousand nurses.

Hospitals are desperate for doctors to take on extra shifts – and pay a premium for those who do. Dr. Liam Brennan, the president of the Royal College of Anaesthetists, told the *Guardian* in April 2017, "Hospitals should not be reduced to begging, but what other option do they have when the NHS is so chronically under-resourced?"

A 2017 NHS analysis found serious shortages of doctors and midwives in maternity wards in Britain. Eighty-eight percent of maternity units were struggling to meet staffing requirements.

The UK government is currently trying to lure 3,200 "physician associates" from the United States by promising them relocation packages with forty-one days paid vacation and a free flight home every year or two.

Hospital beds, too, are in short supply. In the past thirty years, the number of beds has declined by half. A report from the King's Fund, a think tank in England, said that the NHS "now has fewer acute hospital beds per person than almost any other comparable health system."

Wait times are abysmal. In December 2017, more than three hundred thousand people waited for more than four hours in emergency departments for care.

In one case, an elderly woman died after spending thirty-five hours on a gurney in an emergency room. Another patient died of an aneurysm in the waiting room.

Like Canada, the United Kingdom suffers from the bizarre phenomenon of "bed blockers" – patients who don't need to be in the hospital but aren't discharged because they have nowhere to go. British authorities say that there has been a 142 percent increase in bed blocking in the past six years.

The crisis in the country's hospitals is so profound that in January 2018, doctors from sixty-eight hospitals wrote Prime Minister Theresa May to inform her that their patients faced an "intolerable" risk of harm. More than 120 patients a day had been forced to receive treatment in hallways; some died prematurely as a result. Many patients had to wait up to twelve hours for a bed following the decision to admit them to the hospital.

The government has even pulled in the Red Cross to help with what Mike Adamson, the charity's chief executive, called a "humanitarian crisis."

As a result, the quality of care in the United Kingdom is far from ideal. The country has the lowest survival rates for colon, lung, and prostate cancer of seven major industrial nations, according to the Centers for Disease Control and Prevention. UK patients also have far higher mortality rates from heart attack and stroke than do patients in the United States.

Going Private

As in Canada, the United Kingdom's efforts to control costs by fiat haven't worked. Between 1997 and 2009, national health spending climbed an average of more than 8 percent a year.

That rate of increase has slowed in recent years. But part of the slowdown may be a function of patients "going private" – paying

---

Whenever governments try to overrule the laws of supply and demand, the results are rationing, shortages, and runaway costs.

---

on their own for treatments they can't get in a timely fashion from the NHS.

One prostate cancer patient told the *Daily Mail* in September 2017 that he shelled out more than $9,000 for what his doctor told him was a "very urgent" surgery because the NHS delayed his procedure multiple times.

Families now spend more than $780 million a year for treatment, thanks to ever increasing wait times. That's up 29 percent from five years ago, according to government data obtained by the *Independent.* The revenue the Royal Marsden Hospital in London took in from private-paying patients doubled between 2010 and 2016 – and now accounts for more than 31 percent of its income, up from 25 percent six years ago.

Incredibly, the reaction to this by some in the United Kingdom has been to call for shutting off these private-sector escape valves to prevent anyone from jumping to the head of the line.

If that happens, Britons will just leave the country. Many already do. In 2016, 144,000 people went abroad to seek medical care – nearly triple the number from two years prior. In some cases, the NHS has gone so far as to offer to pay for patients to receive treatment in Calais, France, on the other side of the English Channel, because it can't meet patients' needs at home.

Around the World – and at Home

Canada and the United Kingdom aren't outliers. Whenever governments try to overrule the laws of supply and demand, the results are rationing, shortages, and runaway costs.

Those concepts may seem foreign to most Americans. But there are several single-payer systems in the United States – and they're plagued by many of the same issues the Canadian and British systems face.

PART II

SINGLE-PAYER IN THE UNITED STATES

America's single-payer programs – Medicare, Medicaid, and the Veterans Health Administration – fail to provide the high-quality care its residents demand.

Medicare and Its Discontents

Let's start with America's first single-payer system, Medicare, which covers more than fifty-seven million people. Since its creation in 1965, the entitlement program has provided government-funded medical coverage to all Americans sixty-five and older. The original program consists of Part A, which covers hospital care with funds collected through a payroll tax on current workers, and Part B, which takes care of visits to doctors and is funded through a combination of premiums and general government revenue.

Medicare has since expanded to cover

younger Americans suffering from long-term disability, end-stage renal disease, and amyotrophic lateral sclerosis, more commonly known as ALS or Lou Gehrig's disease.

As of 1997, beneficiaries can also purchase privately administered Part C, or Medicare Advantage, plans as an alternative to parts A and B. In 2003, President George W. Bush signed a law creating Medicare Part D, which provides seniors subsidized prescription drug coverage.

Like countless other government-run health insurance schemes, Medicare's costs have exceeded its funding in all but two of its years in existence. It's made up the difference by borrowing from other federal programs. An analysis coauthored by former Congressional Budget Office director Douglas Holtz-Eakin put the program's 2016 cash shortfall at $349 billion.

Decades of cost overruns have made Medicare the single-biggest contributor to the national debt; it now accounts for one-third of that debt. By 2029, Medicare Part A's trust fund will be bankrupt, according to the latest report from the program's trustees.

Officials in the United States have responded to this cost crisis just as their counterparts in Canada and the United Kingdom have – by effectively rationing care.

In 2015 alone, Medicare underpaid hospitals by $41.6 billion. Faced with the prospect of losing money treating Medicare patients, some health care providers are opting out of the program. In 2012, nearly ten thousand physicians did so. That's almost triple the number who opted out three years earlier.

Nearly 14 percent of doctors said in 2016 they would not see patients covered by the program, according to the Physicians Foundation. Another 13 percent admit to limiting the number of Medicare beneficiaries they accept.

By underpaying doctors, Medicare limits seniors' ability to access medical care – the very definition of rationing.

The problem will only grow worse. By

2040, 90 percent of home health agencies, 70 percent of skilled nursing facilities, and half of all hospitals will lose money on Medicare patients.

This is Medicare as we know it – a program barreling toward bankruptcy that copes with its funding crisis by restricting access to care for millions of Americans.

Is this the program progressives want to foist upon the entire country?

Medicaid Is Worse Than Nothing

America's second single-payer system, Medicaid, offers even worse care. Created as part of the same 1965 package that gave Americans Medicare, the entitlement was originally intended to fund basic medical care for low-income patients. Unlike its counterpart, Medicaid is a joint federal-state initiative. States administer the program and receive at least one dollar in federal funding for every dollar they spend on it.

Over the years, the program has grown into the largest provider of health coverage in the United States. Today, Medicaid covers one in five Americans – roughly seventy-four million people – and accounts for one of every six dollars spent on health care in this country.

The most recent expansion of the program

A November 2017 study found that Medicaid offered little-to-no benefit over no insurance for patients with colorectal cancer and melanoma.

---

came under Obamacare, which instructed states to enroll everyone earning less than 138 percent of the federal poverty level. The federal government offered to cover the cost for these newly eligible enrollees between 2014 and 2016. In 2017, states became responsible for 5 percent of the cost of expansion enrollees; that share will rise to 10 percent by 2020.

The US Supreme Court ruled in 2012 that the federal government could not force states to expand Medicaid. Thirty-one states and the District of Columbia did so anyway. In November 2017, Maine's voters approved a ballot measure that directed state leaders to expand the program as well – the first time Medicaid was expanded via public referendum.

All told, fifteen million people nationwide have received coverage thanks to the expansion.

States had difficulty paying for Medicaid pre-Obamacare. The expansion has exacerbated those problems. Since the expansion took effect, both the rate of enrollment and the per-enrollee costs for expansion patients have vastly exceeded the government's initial estimates.

A 2018 report from the Foundation for Government Accountability found that in thirty-one expansion states, enrollment of able-bodied adults in Medicaid was more than double what was anticipated. And while federal officials estimated that costs for newly eligible Medicaid beneficiaries would be about 30 percent less than for those who were previously eligible, the opposite has proven true. In 2015, the cost per expansion enrollee was $6,366 – 23 percent greater than the per-enrollee cost for those who were not part of the expansion population.

Medicaid's total price tag is expected to grow from $575.9 billion in 2016 to $957.5 billion in 2025. States can expect their Medicaid spending to jump by 5.2 percent from 2017 to 2018 alone. Even the Obama administration warned that Medicaid is on track to "displace spending in other important programs" in its final actuarial report on the entitlement.

States struggling to deal with these expenses are simply limiting access to care. About 650,000 people are currently on waiting lists for Medicaid coverage. Some states are contemplating work requirements for the able-bodied, to try to reserve the program for those truly in need.

Most states already pay doctors so little that they refuse to see Medicaid patients – an indirect form of rationing.

A 2015 study published in the *Annals of Internal Medicine* found that more than thirty state Medicaid programs limited access to expensive drugs that could cure hepatitis C. "I think there is evidence that they are rationing based on cost," said Robert Greenwald, a professor at Harvard and one of the study's authors.

The American Hospital Association reports that hospitals received 90 cents for every dollar they spent treating Medicaid patients. According to the Kaiser Family Foundation, Medicaid reimbursement rates nationwide are, on average, less than three-fourths of Medicare's rates. Medicare's rates, in turn, are lower than those for private insurance.

Consequently, a growing number of doctors are refusing to accept Medicaid patients.

The physician recruitment firm Merritt Hawkins found that just 53 percent of doctors in fifteen large metropolitan areas took Medicaid patients in 2017.

The federal government most recently surveyed Medicaid's rate of acceptance in 2013, before Obamacare's expansion of the program. It found that 68.9 percent of physicians were taking new Medicaid patients. In New Jersey, less than 39 percent took new patients – the lowest share in the country. It should be no surprise that the Garden State's Medicaid reimbursement rates are just 42 percent of Medicare's.

When Medicaid beneficiaries can't get an appointment with a doctor, they turn to the emergency room. Indeed, according to a June 2017 study published in the *Annals of Emergency Medicine*, ER visits increased in states that expanded Medicaid under Obamacare.

A *New England Journal of Medicine* study of an expansion of Medicaid in Oregon that was similar to Obamacare's yielded similar results.

ER visits increased 40 percent in the fifteen months after the state expanded the program.

Perhaps most damning are the data on Medicaid's outcomes. Research has shown that the program's beneficiaries fare no better on several measures of health than people without insurance.

A two-year study of Oregon's Medicaid program compared patients who had been randomly selected for Medicaid coverage through a statewide lottery with individuals who weren't picked – the equivalent of a randomized control study. Researchers found that the Medicaid population showed "no significant improvements in measured physical health outcomes" compared to uninsured patients.

There's even evidence that people on Medicaid are more vulnerable to certain health problems than those without insurance. A study published in the journal *Cancer* looked at patients undergoing surgery for colon cancer – and discovered that Medicaid beneficiaries were more likely to die or experience complications than those without coverage.

A University of Virginia study, meanwhile, revealed that in-hospital mortality rates were higher for surgical patients with Medicaid than for those lacking coverage.

A November 2017 study published by the *Journal of the American Medical Association Oncology* evaluated cancer survival data for patients with varying types of insurance in California. It found that Medicaid offered little-to-no benefit over no insurance for patients with colorectal cancer and melanoma. The six authors concluded that Medicaid offered cancer patients "persistently inferior" outcomes.

In other words, state and federal governments spend more than half a trillion dollars a year on a program that fails to improve the health of its enrollees – or worse, undermines it.

For years, the single-payer health care system operated by the Veterans Health Administration has been a regular source of scandal and embarrassment. Veterans routinely face lengthy delays that compromise their health – and in some cases, their lives.

A review of the VA medical center in Phoenix conducted in 2016 found that more than two hundred patients died while waiting for care in 2015. More than a hundred died while waiting over a nine-month period in 2015 in Los Angeles.

Sadly, health care workers at VA facilities have proven more eager to cover up delays than fix them. In 2014, the agency's inspector general revealed that employees at more than one hundred VA facilities had manipulated wait-time data to conceal the extent of the problem.

That scandal sparked a public outcry and an aggressive $15 billion reform effort in Congress. But the VA is still a mess.

Houston's VA facility was caught falsifying wait-time records well into 2015. The same was true for at least a dozen VA facilities across Virginia and North Carolina. According to a March 2017 investigation by *USA Today*, at least 36 percent of veterans waited more than thirty days to see a mental health professional. The VA scheduling system showed that only 10 percent of veterans waited that long.

Some veterans have been able to seek care in the private sector through the Veterans Choice Program, created in 2014 as part of the Veterans Choice and Accountability Act. The bill poured $16 billion into the VA, including $2.5 billion earmarked for hiring more doctors, nurses, and other medical staff.

Little has changed. The VA has roughly the same number of staff it was expected to have if the $2.5 billion had never been appropriated, according to a recent NPR investigation. Worse, the facilities with new hires did not see any improvement in wait times.

Meanwhile, those veterans who have received permission to seek care outside the VA face "cumbersome authorization and scheduling procedures," according to the VA inspector general. Patients wait an average of forty-five days for care through the Choice program – even though the express purpose of the initiative is to allow veterans to seek private care if they're facing a wait of more than thirty days inside the VA system.

Laboratories of Socialized Medicine

Several states have their own history with single-payer. Fortunately, every state-level single-payer initiative thus far has failed to launch.

Vermont abandoned its drive in December 2014 after getting a look at the price tag. Then-governor Peter Shumlin concluded that the proposed 11.5 percent payroll tax and 9.5 percent state income tax required to fund the overhaul "might hurt our economy."

A Colorado ballot initiative that would have created a single-payer system fell victim to similar cost concerns in 2016. Known as

> *The American people haven't yet grasped what the Bernie Sanders plan would mean for them. Forty-seven percent think they'll be able to keep their current insurance plans under single-payer.*

Amendment 69, the measure would have effectively ended private insurance in the state and replaced it with a publicly funded program dubbed ColoradoCare.

The annual cost to taxpayers? Thirty-six billion dollars – more than the state's entire budget. Democratic governor John Hickenlooper discouraged Coloradoans from voting for the initiative, and they rejected it by an 80-to-20 margin.

Still other state-level single-payer efforts remain alive. In June 2017, the California State senate passed SB 562, which would force all Californians – including those covered by Medicare and Medi-Cal, the state's version of Medicaid – into a single, state-run health care system.

The state senate's Appropriations Committee estimated the annual cost of the bill at $400 billion – more than double California's budget. A study by University of Massachusetts Amherst economist and supporter of the plan Robert Pollin and colleagues, who support the plan, pegged its cost at $331 billion, thanks to a raft of "savings" that amount to little more than proposed price controls on drugs and doctor services.

In late June 2017, Assembly Speaker Anthony Rendon, a Democrat, put the plan on hold "until further notice," calling it "woefully incomplete." Six months later, the bill remained on ice. "Absolutely nothing has happened with the bill," Rendon said in December 2017.

New York's state assembly passed a single-payer bill in May 2017. That measure, which would also replace private insurance with a state-administered health plan, would cost an estimated $226 billion by 2019 – considerably more than the $72 billion the state collects in taxes each year. The state senate did not take up the legislation before adjourning for the year.

Massachusetts took a step toward single-payer in November 2017, when the state senate ordered a study of how much it would cost the Bay State to install such a system. If the cost is deemed lower than the status quo, then the state will have to begin transitioning to single-payer. In January 2018, lawmakers in Rhode Island and New Hampshire also took first steps toward installing single-payer systems in their states.

Government-run health care remains a hobbyhorse for Democrats across the nation – one they are unlikely to dismount anytime soon.

PART III

SINGLE-PAYER PLANS UNDER CONSIDERATION

Single-payer has failed abroad and at home. Yet the call for single-payer from progressives has never been louder.

Vermont senator Bernie Sanders (I-VT) and his dedicated followers have been the loudest. In his campaign for the Democratic presidential nomination in 2016, he promised "Medicare for All." In September 2017, he and sixteen cosponsors – including four likely to seek the Democratic nomination for president – released a bill fleshing out some of the details of his plan. And on January 23, 2018, he held an online town hall meeting watched by over one million people to stump for single-payer.

Unlike Anything in the World

The first thing to understand about Sanders's Medicare for All plan is that it's not simply an expanded version of the existing Medicare program. It's much bigger. In fact, no country has a government-run health care system as all-encompassing and generous as the one Sanders proposes.

Medicare for All would cover everything from hospitalization and doctor visits to vision checkups and mental health care, free of charge.

Well, almost free – patients would be responsible for up to $250 out of pocket for prescription drugs.

There would be no provider lists, no need for referrals. Private insurance would be effectively outlawed; no insurer would be allowed to cover any of the benefits offered by Medicare.

The Sanders plan would upend the health care marketplace in just four years. In year one, anyone fifty-five or older as well as children up to age eighteen could sign up for Medicare. In years two and three, the age limit would drop to thirty-five. And in year four, everyone would be enrolled in the new program.

The American people haven't yet grasped what the Sanders plan would mean for them. Forty-seven percent think they'll be able to keep their current insurance plans under single-payer.

Incalculable Costs

The Sanders plan is clear on what it will cover. It's a lot less clear on how it will pay for it.

"Rather than give a detailed proposal ... we'd rather give the American people options," Sanders told the *Washington Post* in September 2017. "We have economists looking at it who are coming up with different numbers."

Consider the plan Sanders proposed during the 2016 presidential campaign, which is similar to the bill he's since introduced in the Senate.

The Sanders campaign claimed that Medicare for All would cost $14 trillion in its first ten years. The Urban Institute, a liberal think tank, calculated the cost at more than twice that – $32 trillion over ten years.

Even that estimate is probably low. History

is littered with examples of government health care programs that have blown past their promised cost.

The administration of President Lyndon Johnson predicted in 1964 that Medicare would cost $12 billion in 1990; the actual cost was nine times that figure.

More recently, in 2010, the Congressional Budget Office pegged the cost of Obamacare at $940 billion over ten years. By 2017, the CBO had revised its ten-year projection of the program's cost to about $2 trillion.

Sanders's plans for coming up with the trillions he needs are similarly divorced from reality.

He has claimed that his bill would yield $6 trillion in savings over its first ten years, in part by paying health care providers less.

He also has posited administrative savings of $500 billion. Those savings will be difficult to realize, given that the total overhead tab for private insurers today is less than half that figure, according to the Centers for Medicare and Medicaid Services.

Sanders has said he could save another $113 billion a year by slashing drug prices. To do that, he would have to cut prices by one-third, since total spending on prescription drugs in 2015 was $325 billion. Cuts of that magnitude would devastate the industry's ability to research and develop the next generation of cures – many of which could reduce long-term health costs.

To make up the rest, he's floated a litany of new taxes, including a 7.5 percent payroll tax on employers and a 4 percent income tax "premium" to be paid by households. A top tax bracket of 52 percent, higher taxes on investment income, and a "wealth tax" on the net worth of the top 0.1 percent are also on the table.

Sanders has also assumed that the federal government would raise an additional $420 billion a year in revenue, as the tax-free compensation that workers once received in the form of health benefits would be subject to tax under his plan.

Medicare for All might be the most brazen attempt at single-payer, and the most unrealistic. But Sanders may also have set a marker that made a stealthier government takeover of our health care system seem downright reasonable by comparison.

Consider the perennial push for a "public option." During the debate over Obamacare, many progressives argued for the creation of a government-run insurer to compete with private plans in the exchanges. The House's version of what became Obamacare included the public option. The Senate's, which eventually prevailed, did not.

A government-run insurer would have the capacity to absorb essentially limitless losses. So it could underprice private insurers and eventually drive them out of the market. The public option would soon be the only option.

That was the point. Yale professor Jacob Hacker, considered the inventor of the idea, said that the goal was to get to single-payer "in a way that we're not going to frighten people into thinking that they're going to lose their private insurance."

In October 2017, the public option surfaced yet again. Democratic senators Tim Kaine and Michael Bennet dropped a bill that would, at first, allow people to buy into Medicare if they had only one choice of insurer – or no choices at all – through Obamacare's insurance exchanges. Slowly but surely, their bill would expand eligibility – until 2023, when

---

A government-run insurer would have the capacity to absorb losses essentially without limit. So it could underprice private insurers and eventually drive them out of the market.

---

anyone would be allowed to buy into Medicare.

Democratic senator Brian Schatz offered his own take on the public option in 2017, proposing legislation that would allow anyone to buy into Medicaid. Conveniently, Schatz has left it to others to figure out how to pay for his bill.

None of these bills is likely to come up for a vote – much less become law – unless Democrats retake control of Congress and the White House. But they make clear to the American people what the Democrats will do if they take back the reins of power, and that completes the government takeover of the US health care system Obamacare started.

CONCLUSION

Single-payer may provide universal coverage. But as the single-payer systems in Canada, the United Kingdom, and the United States prove, a person who has coverage doesn't necessarily have access to care.

A yearlong wait for treatment from a Canadian specialist doesn't constitute access. As recently retired chief justice Beverley McLachlin of Canada's Supreme Court wrote in the 2005 decision overturning Quebec's ban on private health insurance, "Access to a waiting list is not access to health care."

The millions of Britons languishing on wait lists would surely agree. So would the thousands of US veterans trapped in the VA – as would the American seniors on Medicare and low-income patients on Medicaid who can't find a doctor.

The US health care system needs reforming. For far too many Americans, health care is inaccessible because it's unaffordable. That lack of affordability can explain America's relatively high number of uninsured.

To improve access, our nation must therefore focus on making care more affordable – without sacrificing the high quality that sets the American system apart.

Single-payer fails that test. "Free" coverage may appear affordable to patients. But it's proven unaffordable for governments and the taxpayers that fund them. Government officials have responded by simply capping supply – that is, by limiting access to care.

Such rationing may be direct – like waiting lists, or refusals to cover expensive drugs – or it may be indirect – in the form of cut-rate payments to health care providers that cause them to work fewer hours or close up shop altogether.

Americans want affordable, accessible, quality health care. Single-payer offers just the opposite. That's the unfortunate, and true, promise of Medicare for All.

First American edition published in 2018 by Encounter Books, an activity of Encounter for Culture and Education, Inc., a nonprofit, tax exempt corporation. Encounter Books website address: www.encounterbooks.com

Manufactured in the United States and printed on acid-free paper. The paper used in this publication meets the minimum requirements of ANSI / NISO z39.48–1992 (R 1997) (*Permanence of Paper*).

FIRST AMERICAN EDITION

LIBRARY OF CONGRESS CATALOGING-IN-PUBLICATION DATA IS AVAILABLE

Names: Pipes, Sally, 1945– author.
Title: The false promise of single-payer healthcare / Sally C. Pipes.
Description: New York : Encounter Books, 2018. |
Series: Encounter broadsides ; 55
Identifiers: LCCN 2018000156 (print) | LCCN 2018000684 (ebook) | ISBN 9781641770040 (ebook) | ISBN 9781641770033 (pbk. : alk. paper)
Subjects: | MESH: Single-Payer System | Health Policy | Health Services Accessibility | United States | Canada | United Kingdom
Classification: LCC RA412.3 (ebook) | LCC RA412.3 (print) |
NLM W 225 AA1 |
DDC 368.38/200681—dc23
LC record available at https://lccn.loc.gov/2018000156

10 9 8 7 6 5 4 3 2 1

SERIES DESIGN BY CARL W. SCARBROUGH